Life Cycle

Poems

by

Dena Rash Guzman

Printed in the United States of America

First Printing 2013
1st Edition

ISBN 978-0-9855291-3-0

Dog On A Chain Press
c/o Beasley Barrenton
503 Silverleaf Rd.
Zionville, NC 28698

For ordering information and all other inquiry:
Address or dogonachainpress@yahoo.com

"Nolite te bastardes carborundorum." Margaret Atwood
The Handmaid's Tale

"Skin 'em alive, and leave them along the trail." Bazzel Bumgarden

To be.

Life Cycle

A good story should take men, a lot of them at once.
Sailors upended. Frenzy in a sinking boat.
Women and children first,
as a gentle captain taps softly for help.
The crew, dear men, slipping under water
in striped shirts, or waiters crying out for their mothers
as the cold drinks them to the bottom.
The salty edge disproves Jesus,
silences the ship's horn.
How do you spell the sound a ship's horn makes?
There is no word for that,
for women and children alone at sea,
the tyrannical hag with one leg taking an aside
because of a book she read.
That whale must be here somewhere. Harkening,
she raises her oar, and drowns hysterical.

Life Cycle

I'm wood-clad, weathered,
gray by snow and sun.
The lights inside my stories flicker.
The moon wanes and fills.
Phases matter little to hours
sidling through rooms,
defining and redefining
by fashion and function my trusses,
my mortise and tenon joints,
the structural frame.
I populate my space in time
as only something necessary will.
In a copse of trees, I cover and nurture
my beholden, my spanning generations.
They inch from cradle to rocking chair
here beneath my hand hewn beams,
crafted to last beyond the end
of a hammer's ring, flesh, or loss.

I decay over decades, but hold.

Life Cycle

our lives veer from need to elegy
we are born worth not a thing
but our own sweet hell-bent will
with which we force out first cries
or absolute goodbyes
country after century
banality or greatness
slurried with time
food/sex/shelter
ants and sand
mice and cheese
the alphabet
toys
bows and arrows
briefcase and train ticket
babies and aprons
battleships for eyes
the chalk and eraser of every little lesson

Life Cycle

When I was little, I was so poor
I wept like a baby in art class.
I was hungry. Underfed.
Teacher showed us Warhol's
32 Campbell's Soup Cans.
I wanted to eat them all,
cheese, tomato rice, clam chowder,
right off the screen.
The projector clicked
slide after slide after slide,
can, can. Can, can. Can.
When I was poor, I was so little
I did not understand
that hunger is a gun.
Center golden banner.
Great As A Sauce, Too!
When I was little, I was so poor
that when our can opener broke,
we couldn't afford to replace it.
Mother pried dinner open
with a knife and a spoon,
cut herself, and cried.

I wanted the slide show back.
I wanted 32 cans of soup.

Life Cycle

turn up the hi-fi slip into tight jeans
shiny plastic lip slicker gloss high beam
a bag of jelly beans a root beer a tear
for your fireman boyfriend somewhere
with some other dream teen finish off
a sweet dime bag and turn the hi-fi
higher put on extra eyeliner black
switch out one song for another
have a fistfight with your brother
stride out the door like a cotton picker
fast so you don't see your mother
slide into the seat of the sweet ride
Daddy bought you bass down
low and treble up high
fly
John Cougar fist pump
out the window trailing behind you

a space pilgrim cherry
flailing shooting star

Life Cycle

I like Georgia ok
said a goose to some other geese
at a migratory pit stop en route to Georgia
and maybe they'll screen Casablanca again at that outdoor mall
in Smyrna
or was it Roswell
that little pond and the kids gave us donuts
that was a nice night
after the show a bunch of us went to a great lake
sweet clematis and grass

Life Cycle

I dressed as the Devil for Halloween that year. When I came
downstairs, there was a knock on the door. I answered, expecting
to greet my friend, but small children were standing there in
costumes. *Trick or treat,* they said. I looked at their father,
shocked. I said, *Oh my God. I forgot it was Halloween.* He
seemed confused. I remembered I was wearing a devil costume:
horns and a tight red velvet jumpsuit. He looked at me darkly.
Hold on, I said. *Let me see what I have in the kitchen.*

I came back with one brand new bag of dried apricots. I didn't
know to which child to give them. How do you choose? The
children walked away with their father, without the apricots.

Life Cycle

I can't conquer scorn for wandering fear.
I'm no patient cow. I'm a shrunken secret

forged in tillies and measures of time,
muscled by walks through the pasture

and by crouching beside old Lou
on cold mornings
to quick squirt her milk

into my pail or my pails. I hate
the castle and the king;
his men and maids

do these terrible things,
such terrible things.

I sip. I spit. I spit. I spit.

Life Cycle

I was only a cold coyote
breathing desert dust,
sharp and gray on a red hill.
You were only another coyote,
head down and tail up,
sniffing a mouthful of kill.

I saw your silence
fifteen yards below me.
You didn't sense
my footfall down the rocks.

You bolted at the sight of my eyes
but came back moonlit brightly,
broached the idea of mating,
a vow I took as ordinary
coyotes do, for I was only.

Life Cycle

We hold hands,
our real hands, after work or winter,
skin holding skin
real and rough as a whole day,
the dross the manicurist sloughs away.

Water on a river rock,
where the shine crowds out the current.
We love makeup and its application,
lukewarm tea or forgotten miso
buried inside our baskets. Lipstick.

Why do we cry when time bites?
There is no wolf to blame, no witch,
no vagabond son of a bitch,
just us, swaggering blind and lined,
the face of a woman from Chernobyl
who refused to leave after the reactor got hot.
St. Helens. Pinatubo.

The steam will make us open and clean
between lonely and Sundays,
a day when some people pray.

Life Cycle

you and me
mouth on mouth
tongue to tongue
in secondhand shirts
in pants your sister gave me
the fasteners of modesty
littered across the house

Life Cycle

Faith is the space
between the flesh of a peach
and the knife.
Faithlessness: a slice
of skin, not peach.

Life Cycle

This is how we forget our ancestors:
some recipes are never written.
This is how my great-grandma made biscuits:
every day of her life, until she couldn't anymore.
This is how she made biscuits:
every day, in a wooden bowl at dawn
for her husband, her many children,
her many, many grandchildren, their children,
her needy friends and relatives,
for people at church, for Christmas,
for Easter, for everything.
Maybe for hobos too. Maybe not.
Maybe in the summer she got faint,
maybe she didn't like to mix biscuits
with her ankles swollen by pregnancy,
or while grieving the loss of a child,
or when she had a cold,
or when she had cried in the night,
and don't we all,
and she couldn't make biscuits at all
after her hip, after she got too old.
She died at 98.

Now, I have the wooden bowl.
It rests on my highest shelf.
When I die, it will be thrown away
because it is cracked nearly in half.

Life Cycle

My sister and I had lice once.

We had long thick hair and our mother
comforted us as they jumped off our heads,
fleeing the shampoo that was killing them.

She scrubbed us, laid us on her lap, each after next,
combing our yards of hair with fine little teeth.

She gave us little combs like hers,
and we played them as little instruments.

Her curling iron brushed and curled
our yards of hair to kill the nits.
She washed our bedding,
put our stuffed animals
in plastic bags in the garage.

They stayed there for two weeks.
We didn't miss them much.
We didn't need to. We had her, her smell.

Perfume and cigarette smoke,
sipping a bottle of Dr. Pepper
from time to time, listening to Oprah

while she went over every last bit of our hair.
She would never have cut it. Not ever.

Life Cycle

Best not to be shot out of orbit
like the rabbit our groundskeeper
shot dead with his practice arrows.

The rabbit was coming home from work,
maybe a day of lettuce nibbling,
dodging traps, and was errantly shot.

He was ready to relax with the wife
and kids. Oh, the wife,
how he loved her fluffy tail,

her haunches and her tits
with all those babies on them.
Maybe a little TV, then baby-making,

but he never made it home.
I helped fricassee him. Salt & butter.
Peas & potatoes. Sweet tea.

Poor thing, there in the skillet
unable to wonder why my
hands were preparing to serve him.

His poor wife and babies,
alone in those coarse woods,
no one to open the jelly jar.

Life Cycle

The poppies I didn't plant again this year,
because they are too hard to harvest.
Last year, I just stood outside at midnight
carving them up with X-Acto knives,
licking the milk off the pods.

Most of them went to seed.

It takes stealth to bleed poppies,
watchfulness too.
Precision to scrape the brown opium.
Fermentation costs age, water, soil.
This is why slave armies of children
lose hands, cut off for our lows.

Life Cycle

Nights we sing our bones to sleep,
then our nerves back from it.
Each day we get a dawning,
a hot cake from the oven.

Life Cycle

Coltrane out the speakers,
a tarantula on the wall.
Tarantulas don't kill people, people do.
I do. Outside the window
space is shattered by impatience.
Slapdash buildings, excess, no masonry.
Cracker boxes and sky above,
the flat world below it, the round one,
its satellites, one livid central flame.

The music swells down
to the scratch of the needle
dancing in the grooves.
I off the switch. The sound dies.
The spider lives.

Life Cycle

My blouse unfastened just above the waist.

The river brimmed at its banks. The moss is a deity that covers all. I know somewhere drums winch out the language of war. My feet scratched up in the after-light, to the house. This is the time of year to revert to history: eat, fuck, sleep.

What breeds in us is dirty and clean.

Life Cycle

an itch somewhere—on a cheek,
a breastbone, elbow or thigh

these are places of instigation,
where the orders between

our desires and our futures
break down, where the heart

gets under our skin and a sense
of pain sets in to hopeful avail

everybody has an itch, or ought to,
for only the itches and the yielding

to them, to their needs, and the way they careen,
can teach us to care enough for our own hands.

Life Cycle

loss reveals itself,

but not uninvited.
I wanted to be polluted
with life,
to host rapid reproduction,

to abide by our
evolutionary duty.

Life Cycle

Courtship

Your friends thought I was very young.
I was, but not that young.
You told me you couldn't stand crazy girls.
That is when I knew you were in love.

Pregnancy

Jesus my belly was huge
and that wasn't all.
My mother said,
she never saw someone
so pregnant her ass looked pregnant, too.
I was drinking whole milk.

Domesticity

I like white porcelain. You hate chips.
I drop dishes when I get upset.
You fold socks or watch the game.
We smell like love together.

Life Cycle

some skipping record, some poster of a girl in a bikini
legs wet hips jutting so her belly becomes a gully
some narrow bed, some subzero air conditioning
blowing powerful away the sweat
we rub against each other but don't admit it
to each other or to anyone else alive
you full of football and pizza and Robitussin
me full of it, full of you, full of bones

Life Cycle

10:07 pm
the grass outside the window
takes on the last of the snow
I taste of cinnamon
under the blanket his hands find a pot of gold
pink jellybean blue ribbon
our teeth meet and flint a forest on fire

10:57 pm
scrambled eggs and beer

8:23 am
fire meets fire

8:57 am
donuts

10:07 am
the snow outside the window hands its ass
to the first of the grass

Life Cycle

Forget the last dinner, how I burdened the strangers beside us
with my need for constant outer dialogue, forget the bad wine.
Remember the smell of the lilac bush outside the window of the
too-small house, the thrift store painting in the hall. We liked it
with voracious eyes, we ate cold sweet porridge out of coffee
cups for breakfast. Hot and not touching beneath our worn sheets
we fell asleep to the sunrise. I hope you forgot the sound of the
door closing behind me, but not the way we laughed at things
such as going without dinner. Remember things that cannot
really die—books and good cheese on payday, philosophy, them
feral cats in in the desert gully. Our only pets.

Life Cycle

You came at me like a yeti.
What hunter of a yeti ever finds a yeti?
They find only nests of splintered
twenty-foot trees, and piles of bones and skins.
You found me, Eve in the stand,
heavily armed and hidden by leaves,
peering out at the wilderness
through binoculars. You were there,
lurking unreal in a forest where the rain never stops.

I didn't believe you were real, but you were,
there always. I saw your tracks first.
Some of them rhymed.
Yetis don't write poetry, do they?

This is why I never heard you coming.
You made like Byron, you animal.

Life Cycle

We did kick through the garden, careless
and I did feel disenchanted and bored.
Most nights, it was dark and quiet.

Days though, I got lost
in greens so green
only a God could have made them.
Black was black, but

my hands hovered over
flowers as
hummingbirds choosing
which to suck, which
to plunder and huff,

my pulse
a tiny heart
falling back through grasses
onto soil loamy soft

soft beneath
our bare skin, beneath
perfect blue
gently clouded skies.

Life Cycle

Last night,
heels askew in the hallway,
I bent in half for him,
held tight the doorknob
while he rode me
like a Mongolian soldier
astride a stolen horse,
fleeing his own army.

Life Cycle

Fight some other to win. Fight. Win.
Manfully, artfully, full of whiskey,
uniform, tanks, rockets. Sound the sirens!
Families swarm, make way for the fury
as we prepare to defeat the enemy.
The toys are on the map. The map is of the world.
The world is of our making.

When you were a child, deer leapt before you,
before your spear and your shirtless fervor.
Now you dream, eyes on high beam,
head set straight on your shoulders.
Baby doll, you want to be a soldier.
This is the tradition, the experience
of survival, a game and a training taking over.

You wore your best Converse
and a shirt with a collar to the recruiting station,
your very best Chucks, hair slick, ears shined.
I let you take our truck.

By the rule of your law, the place you occupy,
the rule of broken rules, economies, civilizations,
you prepare, hope glimmering at the tip of your spear,
trained on victory and survival as if it will hold you.

Life Cycle

I'll sit
on the curb in the rain
and flip out
near Chinatown,
coffee and donuts
in steed of absinthe.
I'll write a poem
about a blurry, blurry
night, smear my lipstick,
then sing the national anthem
before cutting off my ear
which I'll post to you,
post to you,
notice I say post.

Life Cycle

All I want to do is make poetry famous. - David Lerner

All I want to do is grip your bust
firm, one arm around your soul,
but not shoulders, such big ones,
and squeeze a little. Marble doesn't
give. The Empire State Building I am

inside my pants won't give an inch
until you get riotously drunk, relax,
and let me hear your poetry naked as
the disregarded, or as lay and lie transposed,
but this, I mean, is not what I mean.

I don't care about your verses now,
only your lava blood rushing rowdy
once more to your broke down heart,
then down lower to your bottom,

and how it knows I kick it out
from under your top, where your bust
of marble cold is hard and still false
everything, yet the one thing ever beloved.

Life Cycle

The first day I saw you
with your mouse dark hair,
your ghost pale skin,
tiny fisted, you grasped one
warm dark hair,
perhaps molecules of still womb air.

Until this day I thought you
(no womb house and more hair,
yet most frail of skin)
a baby still, a persistent one
of mouse hair,
but you grew by molecules of new toy air.

Each day now I'll watch you,
still black mouse of dark hair,
grow into a sail of skin
and move unassisted and up as one
with your full gift of hair
to create a wake of molecules of air.

Life Cycle

The way I'd hold his big hand
between my own bantam ones and squeeze
to keep him put wasn't nice
and didn't work.
He was already gone,
like stolen money or an AWOL private
off the back of a truck,
too afraid of the war to really go.

Life Cycle

We are not wealthy.
No gems stitched into my hems.
No gold. No booty. No dinner.
Nobody here ever was shanghaied.

Seafaring? I'd sink. I'm 10,000 tons of lead.

When my ship arrives it'll be full of alien life,
eyes for weapons, crop circle tattoos.
Mom. They all will represent Mom.
Or anchors. Aliens love anchors and moms.
The ink will color us burnt sienna—
dead. A bomb too big to comprehend.

I am broke and unhinged. Gravedigger dirty.
Tinpot as a skinned raccoon. Fat carton of spoiled milk.
I am just a beggarly man on the lam, up a staircase,
a flat-footed cop waddling in chase.
Criminal on the roof, he yells. *Come down!*
I can't give up now.
I can't afford the ticket.

Life Cycle

Falling in love is like a hungry cat.
Or, maybe not. You can just feed the cat.
Then it shuts up and sleeps.
Falling involves a floor,
even if the floor is under a mattress.
When the cat gets hungry again,
feed it your bootstraps.
Love is hungrier than that.
Pull yourself up by the ponytail,
or drink cognac on the floor.

Life Cycle

We live just over the right side of the tracks. I still say we live here, even though you are gone. The trains all but run through our side yard. The ones that don't slow down on their way past never catch my notice. It's the ones that stop that wake me from my mourning and interfere with my reverie. If I'm sleeping, I wake up. If I'm doing anything else, I stop. I can barely just see the platform from the bathroom window. I run to look at the passengers getting off of every passenger train. I hold my breath as long as I can, imagining that if I can hold it till the last person steps down that the last person will be you. I make bargains with God. *If I can count to 100 before the tenth passenger is greeted by someone, he'll be on this train.*

It never works.

Life Cycle

You want me
but you want something else
so change me
into a good book
a beach hut
rice and wine
a philosopher
a war king
your waitress
your favorite one
with the plump behind
that feeds your eyes
the cheeseburger of your childhood dreams
more hot coffee
shelter from hunger
Cutty Sark.
Flour with heat and yeast and salt; bread.
Cotton.
I can be soft blankets
a cookie baker
a banker
but no matter what, I will always hate *Breakfast at Tiffany's*.

Life Cycle

I think she's kind of ugly.
Her voice on water
comes across the table,
seething round the rim of her glass.
The waiter: more water, no ice.
Her voice on no ice is colder.
The starch between us, miles of muslin tundra.

She likes the frost, the rot underneath
when the sun comes around again.
Him. There is no him.

He vanishes into each year,
bloody and more lavish
than a golden coke spoon.

Her breasts quiver in their sweet cage.
I prickle at their salute. I fuck off.

Life Cycle

deal with the man
get snubbed

define the short version of a long hoax
he is a heavy load, I am a faulty wheel

the burden of my body on his ego
the burden of his ego on my body

repair my bike, make it purr
I'm a pioneer, motherfucker

pack it up and move along
be deadly for one entire day

stop at the roadside, eat a salad
shoot at interlopers, scare them off

use suburban words to express country concepts
dare to allow the years to pile up

dare not to die, not today
consider the audacity

decide to eat unagi hotdogs
remember the man, lose my appetite

memorize Molly Bloom's soliloquy
recite it to the other pioneers

call shenanigans
call a friend

tell him he's charming but hard to read
tell him he's James Joyce

tell him yes instead of no

tell him everything has changed

tell him to tell me what he knows
tell him charming is for waiters

tell him he'll have to wait
wait for him to wait

forget who's waiting, grow drowsy
set the alarm, go to sleep cold

33 degrees

Life Cycle

I am boxing ring bruised,
but not a springboard for your autocracy,
not a gift with purchase.

Most unwelcome,
you are nothing, not a bee
beckoned by a wax mouth dark flower.

Life Cycle

to Tim, who nearly died today

I've had all my life
to compose these little poems.
Sun like a vowel,
pancakes and departure,
a dawn of truth, farewell at the door,
bus after car. It goes and goes on.

Every day like coffee,
plain as black, no cream.

Each light, each blue,
every leaf I've seen
comes on, barely green,
to burn away its new
to its last time on the line,
as fire gold red orange,
down to nothing
but a gray plea for
anything again.

But Tim it was you,
before the fire that
never came,
gap-toothed grin and
axe in hand, chopping
away the blackberries
until you dropped in a grip
of fierce heart-killing pain,
carried by Billy to the doctor
and then by the ambulance
to the hospital in the rain;
it was you who
prevented me from
spoiling the paper with
any more mixed metaphor

or misplaced assonance—
this is the nature of
sudden dissonance.

The sun is unlike a vowel.
Black coffee is anything but plain.

That last breath that came again
at the restart of your heart
is the only poetry this day,
come pancakes or departure,
can rightly proclaim.

Life Cycle

As I walked out on everything,
it rained in drafts, in edits,
angry bursts of shorthand.

It was June or January -
I could not own the dates,
could not take them for drinks,
could not forget the folly
of trusting a weasel with hens
for even one moment.

Art of War, red shoes, suitcase.
I walked out on everything.

Life Cycle

moonfaced baby at breast,
milk for lunch in Shanghai,
curled in a one arm cradle,
one baby blue baby shoe over mother's elbow.
mother at the cart under a tree in the rainy sunlit leaf shadow,
cooking with her free arm.
moonfaced baby is fat.

mother mother mother

inside me, a pull. I want to take the baby
hold him, feed him rice from a bowl,
buy him milk in a box,
give him a bath,
rock him until his caterpillar lashes
shut to dreams.

mother mother mother

baby eyes me, little smile, breast milk moon-cheek.
moonface baby twists, still latched, to see me better.
mother winces, eyes me too.

moon-baby's mother thrusts a bowl at me,
one-handed. I am free.
I eat my rice and meat,
moon-cheek free, alone.

Life Cycle

I saw two very old Chinese men in Zhongshan suits
at a Lunar New Year champagne brunch
at the Shanghai Westin. Champagne, after coffee.
Next, more coffee, then unbridled delight over the entertainment:
acrobats and arias. *if energy ceases, ghosts will come*
I watched them through their clouds of smoke,
my own mimosa-drunk gaze as they laughed,
then smoked again. Chung Hua.
The lobby shone around us as a fishbowl,
inverted soaking color and bright-tailed women
circling like fish, pouring limitless champagne.
if replenishment ceases, ghosts will come
Those men came in weathered faces,
starched, brand new suits in Mao's old style,
in old age, in steel and soon enough death,
skin like a road map of Puxi, sons in Armani.
if wakefulness ceases, ghosts will come, will come
I, feasted and heavy with the punctuation
of last night's fireworks on my dreams, heard them speak.

Hong bao na lai. Did you ever see this coming?

Life Cycle

labor camps posted as communes—slave labor,
just a peasant, long illegal now, and before japanese
occupation, so mao said they had too much food. he
shut the canteens, cut off noses for harvesting the harvest.

steal food, even unripe, time and again they will.
I can't stand the houses. he said. chinese architecture
is most delightful when torn to the ground like this,
and he snapped, and tanks shot concrete like semen

impregnating the concrete with more concrete
as people starved in the city, and nationwide, reported
a famine witness in peking, dejection in each county,
each village, each home where all the children died

eating pond scum, needing rice. aesthetics.
this is why they died, like how the mao souvenir
alarm clock will never tell time, engineered
wrong on purpose. tens of millions of people.

Life Cycle

Tea leaves us fortified
but knowing

only our red bird hearts
beating oolong-stained
in fine bone cups.

Life Cycle

In Soo Chin's garden
honeysuckle vines choked a
fronded mesquite.

I absorbed the last starlight
of the year. Soo Chin brought
tea and confusing wisdom.

"My grandson is not your mirror.
He'll see that when his eyes turn
inward. When I was a boy in China
I loved a good woman too, but I
married Mrs. Chin instead."

All around us the New Year gathered.
Rain whispered miles high in clouds
we would never know.

Life Cycle

Cheap shoes
and blisters with miles to go,
a courtyard path grown over.
The disaster we were
is a bad metaphor
for hard love.
Good luck scorns me.

Life Cycle

I fell asleep in a skirt and heels, walked pretty in dreams.
Upon waking, mascara spiders nest in my fine lines.
I ask the man beside me to leave.
Change into pajamas, turn on the laptop, click Photos.
You. You. You. I, I, I.
A Bangkok monk with a metal bowl for alms.
I look at my ceramic bowl of oatmeal, back to the screen.
Street animals in Thailand. Soi dogs.
They slept in gutters and were dirty but tame.
I shut it down, stand up.
I wash away the spiders. The man leaves.
I eat the oatmeal. I do pushups. I read the news.
I liked the street animals. I liked the street animals.
I liked the street animals in Thailand.

They were dirty but tame.

Life Cycle

I can't be cruel to you, Godzilla.

I can't send you poisoned letters
stamped with pluming skulls and bones.
I can't send you love notes or gifts, either.
I have no address for you but the sea,
no paper big enough for your claws.
No mailman would dare deliver
something as it never was,
something as it never can be.

I hear you coming.
You do not die. You do not die.
You regenerate.
A beating heart is all it takes.

My shame is deep,
human intervention
with elemental being.
Look closely and breathe slowly,
sans atomic breath/nuclear beam/radioactive ray.
Good Godzilla, can I just call you Ray?
Between the buildings
are spaces made for your steps.
Tread gingerly to me.
I'll paint my lips for you,
lean out the 21st story window,
stop the massacre with my skirts
and cookies, all my little promises.

Life Cycle

Come on, healing powers.
Come on, oxycodone.
Hillbilly heroin.
Six inch scar.
Wolverine, you lucky dog.

Life Cycles

I don't know who will love me
when I can't read anymore, can't dance funny,
buy a new hat, go outside to see spring's leaves
explode into life one by one,
by god or science or happenstance,

when I can no longer argue that nothing happens for a reason,
that reason is human and everyone knows humans
aren't of earth but just relics of a horrible accident
in which a large alien ship crashed somewhere in Africa,

when I am anything but pretty,
when my skin is only wrinkles and spots
and pink abrasions and my eyes are foggier
than the California coast in the morning,

when I don't remember what a clock is for,
when a meal is a can of Ensure and some soft carrots
cooked in a factory and reheated by a morose dietician,

eaten alone with no one to ask me who loves me,
but I am afraid to ask any elderly person,

Who loves you? Who hasn't died before you?
Does it matter? Do you wish your mother was here?
Do you wish someone would carry you
to the fields where you played softball
in a loose cotton dress and no shoes
every sunny summer day until dinnertime?

Life Cycle

I don't know how to say. How?
If it's not a planet eating a planet,
it's a tornado, food poisoning, a gun.
Somewhere a bride is crying,
heaving her breasts, giving up.
You know what's out there,
stroking you without touch,
like angels watching you struggle
to reach the itch where soon a tattoo.

This is why you do not sleep.
At night the silence in your ears
makes mine ring. A simple statement
you sent, smoke signal or text.
I'm bad. Had good night.
Call me. You ring.
I'm making toast. I leave it
in the toaster, eat the butter
finger by finger by finger
until I bite myself on purpose.

The world holds you to it far, not near.
I tell you no more beer.
I make kale and coffee. I ward
off cancer cells by caffeine,
with greens, by saying cancer is not real.

What do you make? Time for me at dawn,
perhaps, as yolk hatches across your sky.
Time zone, time zone.
Time. I can't know what you can't know,
but I tell you we'll be fine. Concrete.
Hätila ragulpr på fåtskliaben.

Life Cycle

The doctor is a poet.
CT scan, biopsy, radiation.
Stage I, II, III. Chemo.
MRI. Tumor, tumor, tumor.
He has the cadence of Roethke.
The doctor is a boxer.
The old one-two, he says.
The doctor is a philosopher.
I ask if the time is now.
Be here now, he says.
The doctor is a gambler.
He puts his cards on the table.
Consultation. The doctor is a doctor.
Treatment, the best treatments,
the only treatments.
Or, no treatment at all.

I am a patient. I close my eyelids,
stay behind them for a week.
I open them. I live another year.

Life Cycle

Pisces Horoscope for December 21, 2012

PISCES: After a long life as the center of the known universe, things are coming to a standstill. Because you are so abnormally full of hope, you didn't listen to your inner Chicken Little, nor did you check the Mayan calendar and see that indeed, we all do die. And now you are going to die and so is everything you know and no amount of Piscean charm or persuasion will stop it. Don't fret, just turn your watery little soul over to fate and eat it up. We are all, after all, made of stars. BEAUTY TIP: don't wear pastels on the last day of everything. Dress in something more dramatic. Wishy washy watercolor fish get washed out by cosmic end-time storms of hell and fury; only great whales in coats of utilitarian custom-tailored blubber and halos of barnacles can swim to the other side without looking a mess.

Life Cycle

Madame Curie pasted herself to element,
heart to the physical world,
to Irene, hungry enriched Irene, glowing.

Foggy agony, the blood of her blood so bright,
blood infected by cups of brilliance,
shining cups of light, her cracked hands poisoned

but once softer, hold Irene's smaller hands.
She is leaving, she is leaving hers to Irene, to all.

Take it with great care. The first, she took her diploma
and with Irene's father, the gold, that element, that prize.
She gave it back to the earth, to us, to all mankind.

The end is the end or the half-life, loves of her life,
of her life, and do you know what she dreamed
last night—her very last night?

She was a chef sautéing mushrooms in the sky.

Life Cycle

The need for translators
will not diminish while the world eats itself to death.
We have to speak to one another in order to consume.

Look from a Romanian title back to the blank screen.
Tell us what it says, in case we need to know.
Make understandable text which was born hard
by fingers from another tongue, make it simple as a grocery list.

The need for poets
will not diminish as the world eats itself to death.
We have to speak to one another in order not to consume.

Life Cycle

If you find me
my bones tossed true
in a cedar grove
at the foot of the bridge
a merit of moss at my feet
a village of fungi in my skull
a family of voles
peeking out a volcano of soil
flowers blossoming where my loins were
you will know I was lost.

Life Cycle

My dead and buried
speak from the memorial cards
inside my white Bible.
They command through their ghost teeth,
Again. Grace! There is no again.
The leaves turn red and turn gold.
I go dark and cold like the snuff
Grandma spit into her tin can.

Life Cycle

I don't take my delight outside
every day and wind it up,
fly it like an airplane,
Amelia Earhart, to exotic lands.
My heart belongs in my hands.

I should dust daily, curious to find
what is clean. I have no control over decay,
but I can sweep.

I drink champagne, brut force
delicious unless I'm downing coffee and
those little jars of pills that multiply.
Then kale, which I never grow or dig myself,
but I eat it because it's radical good,
like in the eighties when L.A. folks did coke,
atoning next day with jogging and sushi.

I will build that tree house, because who else;
a three story yurt 120 feet up in some old growth fir,
for how little we matter at the end of an hour.

Life Cycle

When I find myself stopping by the woods
over and over, trees bald and still,
stuck between the white ground and gray sky,
arrows through a plank, I am not there at all.
It is because I covet the smoothness of you on my teeth.

What I do well, I want. What I do better, I stop.
I am noon-day clear but reeling, hot on the clutch.
Tuck in your letters, your mania, your triggers.
If a roughness has entered me, your fingers put it there.

Take a good look at that gift.

Life Cycle

This morning the sun lights fire to my eyelashes.
That leaded window glass has done this to the slumbering
since the 1930s. This wall is the sole spot against which a
bed can be placed. In it, I feel the outline of nearly a century's
worth of bodies dreaming.

This morning I hear singing in the fields.
A rooster boasts.
A small plane drones overhead.
I imagine the pilot landing, desperate.

Behind this house; pines
for forty miles, until the volcano.
After that, more. Then, the desert.

The coyotes circle the farm at night.
I know why they howl.
The deer know, too.

Life Cycle

gentlemen and ladies hunt
as bears do for salmon on steps
where the river meets the sea in Alaska
chew only the skin—leave the flesh for the birds

with attachment comes little chats across the table
uglier some dawns than by the easy nights
across the eggs or cereal or thick coffee
sometimes dumplings—sometimes nothing

she says *why don't you stay awhile*
she says *I have a bet to place*
he says *you look afraid*
she says *I am afraid*

Life Cycle

He woke from a deep sleep,
cheek deep in slobber with a
throbbing between his eyes.

He dreamt he sailed
into the heart of Rome,
a wailing wind behind his bailing
back, pushing—the rocks were
deep beneath the rolling blue,

the woman on his deck useless
but for looks. Mexican.
High on Coke. She spoke.
Te quiero con locura.

He wondered at what people will savor,
will pay for this, for the weak flavor
and what comes after the blinding mirage

where mermaids sing. *There's a
band tonight. Get up. Get up.*

Then, laughter.

Life Cycle

our lives wove north in
long lines. *hurry.*
our going formed a steady wreath of
air traffic. come home soon. *we miss you.*
fellow passengers travel with their own discrepancies.
some, the very young or illicitly in love,
do not even realize they have any. *it's good to see you.*
we are contoured or worn away by the wind
over the wings or the rush of asphalt pooling
behind us as miles of inky ribbon. *i love you.*

   i love you.

rise up through the atmosphere, the sun on you
is a new bride's diamond—
sharp.

steady now. leave the earth, fauna, streams, juncture.
burn rubber, make haste. *welcome home.*

Life Cycle

a little to the left
there, there
stop at the light and dig
it's what makes night into night
it's not the darkness at all
it's the electricity
the static colors
coming neon out of your mouth
love is not frivolous
the itch is there
there, there
harder. up. it burns.
a molotov martini
and I could never
reach it without you

Born in Las Vegas and named for Dean Martin, **Dena Rash Guzman** was once exiled to China, but now lives on the organic family farm near Portland, Oregon. After years of vigilance, Dena has obtained conclusive poetic evidence that a juvenile Sasquatch resides in the cedar grove near the lower forty. That evidence is embedded within these pages. She drinks Bulleit whiskey for breakfast, coffee before bed, and imports quinoa and coconut water to make the ends meet.

Photo: **Gabriel Santerno**

Cover art and design: **W. M. Butler**

Previous publishers of some of these poems, in whole or in part, or under other titles, include Ink Node (USA); Cha: An Asian Literary Journal (Hong Kong); Unshod Quills (USA); Gertrude (USA); HALiterature (People's Republic of China and USA); Fried Chicken and Coffee (USA); Hobo Camp Review (USA); Thrush Poetry Journal (USA); The Santa Fe Literary Review (USA); Far Enough East (People's Republic of China); Shanghai 24/7 (People's Republic of China); You've Been Eaten By A Hamburger Zine (USA); Smalldoggies Magazine (USA); Luciole Press (USA);The Las Vegas Poets Society (USA); and Fork Burke (Switzerland.)

The poem *Life Cycle*, previously published by Ink Node under the title *32 Warhol*, was produced as a film in 2013 by filmmaker Jerimiah Whitlock. For the film, it was translated to German and narrated by Bjorn Wahlstrom.
The poem *Life Cycle*, previously published by Ink Node under the title *On The Stars Outside*, was produced as a film in 2012 by filmmaker Swoon.

The poem *Life Cycle*, previously published by Ink Node under the title *An Itch Somewhere*, was written after Robert Michael Pyle's essay on ditches in Thunder Tree: Lessons From an Urban Wildland.
In the poem *Life Cycle*, the line "All I want to do is make poetry famous" was taken from the poem *Mein Kampf* by David Lerner, as it appeared in the book The Outlaw Bible of American Poetry, Basic Books, 1999

From the bunker:

There are poetry people, there is poetry for people and people for poetry. There is all of that other stuff as well, but this is no place for that. Dena Rash Guzman is that poetry and she writes what she writes because she is those people and she is her poetry. That's what mattered to me when deciding to take on this project with her, and I of course found out even more, perhaps the inevitable more than I would of imagined, but that is not me, I expect that and if I don't feel that such is possible…well, someone else can do the book. This project was/is and promises to continue to be a veracious collaboration; of art and form, person and content, element and force, one that damn near softened me to its own comforting belly, but that is not me, of course I could elaborate and carry on with grandiose, but this is no place for that. DRG knows where I am if she wants the brutal truth, the gospel that is…real life shit, although I know she is already fully aware of these Life Cycles that have born us to this world, given us our fight, and given us our name. Dena is who we are in every regard.

Keep a lantern lit.

Beasley Barrenton
Editor/Bomb Shelter Maintenance: Dog On A Chain Press

We would like to raise a glass (or a mason jar) and extend a gallant praise to all of those that have hunkered down and helped us feed the hyena.

And for everyone else that keeps us together and supports what we do…an ever growing colossus of companions and to whom we give our greatest gratitude, you are who we are. Viva La!!!

"The subtle apocalypse we all dream of."

www.ingramcontent.com/pod-product-compliance
Lightning Source LLC
Chambersburg PA
CBHW030006311025
34790CB00039B/658